+

IMPRIMAT

Kathy L

The Child w

Learns The Faith

+

NIHIL OBSTAT

Given at Harrisburg, PA on the 20th of October, 2006 by
Carol L. Houghton, STD, JCD, Censor librorum

+

IMPRIMATUR

Given at Harrisburg, PA on the 20th of October, 2006 by
The Most Reverend Kevin C. Rhoades, Bishop of Harrisburg

"I happily recommend this book, THE CHILD WITH AUTISM LEARNS THE FAITH. The author faithfully and creatively presents the early stories of Sacred Scripture using teaching methods that help children with autism learn the Biblical stories and their message for today. It is so vitally important that we have good and effective catechetical resources for children with disabilities. I am deeply grateful for Kathy Labosh's service to the Church in writing this excellent book to assist teachers and parents in sharing the faith with children with autism."

—The Most Reverend Kevin C. Rhoades, Bishop of Harrisburg

Praise for Kathy Labosh's
The Child with Autism
Booklet Series

Praise for Kathy Labosh's
The Child with Autism
Learns The Faith

"Just when you thought Kathy Labosh's THE CHILD WITH AUTISM series couldn't get any better, along comes another remarkable book for parents and educators of children with autism: THE CHILD WITH AUTISM LEARNS THE FAITH is a comprehensive step-by-step guide to enriching the lives of children through religious education. Using a Judeo-Christian model as her foundation, Labosh presents biblical stories in meaningful, bite-size segments that children of all ages and abilities can relate to. Creative hands-on activities, catchy songs and memorable daily prayers compliment each lively lesson.

"Besides serving as a testament to Labosh's education and sensitivity, the author's incorporation of Jewish references and Hebrew terminology makes THE CHILD WITH AUTISM LEARNS THE FAITH appealing to members of the Jewish community at large. It is an indispensable reference tool for any parent and educator who believes in the timeless values, lessons and mores inherent in religious history and practice. Kudos to Labosh for filling such a vital need within the exceptional community."

- Aviva Engel, Editor, EXCEPTIONAL FAMILY

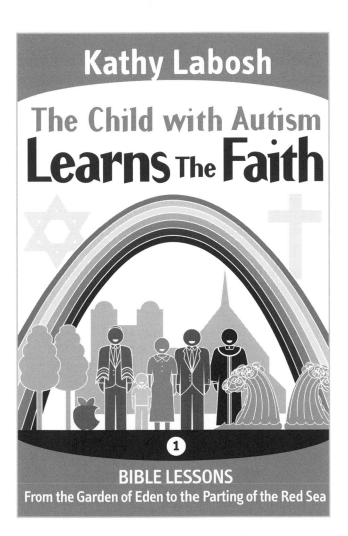

Kathy Labosh

The Child with Autism
Learns The Faith

1

BIBLE LESSONS
From the Garden of Eden to the Parting of the Red Sea

A part of The Child with Autism series

LABOSH
BOOKLETS

East Petersburg, Pennsylvania

www.laboshpublishing.com

The Child with Autism Learns the Faith: Book 1
BIBLE LESSONS From the Garden of Eden to the Parting of the Red Sea
By Kathy Labosh
Published by Labosh Publishing. A part of The Child with Autism series of booklets
PO Box 588, East Petersburg, PA 17520-0588
www.laboshpublishing.com / email: info@laboshpublishing.com

All scripture readings come from The New American Bible, Copyright 1987 World Bible Publishers revised 1991 unless otherwise noted.

Disclaimer: Please note that the materials contained in this booklet are based on the author's own experiences and/or information obtained by the author from other sources. The booklet is for informational purposes only. The reader is advised to use his or her own judgment in applying the information to the reader's own situation and care of his or her children. This booklet cannot be construed as providing any medical, health, legal, child, or product safety advice. All company and product names, logos or trademarks included in this book are exclusive property of their respective holders.

Cover and Interior Book Design by Pneuma Books, LLC
For more info, visit www. pneumabooks.com

ISBN 0-9744341-4-0
ISBN 13: 978-0-9744341-4-8
LCCN: 2006907035

Printed in the United States on acid-free paper by UGI

11 10 09 08 07 06   6 5 4 3 2 1

This booklet and all Labosh Booklets are available in quantity discount for distribution and premium offers. If you are an association, organization, corporation, or individual and you would like to partner with Labosh Publishing to help people with autism and their loved ones, please contact Labosh Publishing at partner@laboshpublishing.com or ask your local autism support group to carry Labosh Booklets. Labosh Booklets are available directly from Labosh Publishing or through your major wholesaler. If you would like to create a custom Labosh Booklet, please contact Labosh Publishing directly. Thank you for your support.

This book is dedicated to Rev. Joseph Celia

1940 - 2005

He loved the flock and the flock loved him.

Table of Contents

Appendices

Foreword

In October 2005, Kathy Labosh presented a remarkable workshop to parishioners and parish staff of the Archdiocese of Philadelphia on partnering in religious education for children with autism spectrum disorders (ASD). Her engaging and humorous style expressed and validated many of the experiences of those workshop participants who were raising a child with ASD. It provided others a glimpse into the lives of families who every day must navigate through an environment not necessarily sensitive to children with ASD.

As members of faith communities we must welcome all members of God's family. To do so, we need greater understanding of all who come to fellowship with us and we must provide opportunities for each person's meaningful participation. Faith communities should strive support the blessings and challenges found in raising children of all abilities.

All people are designed for spiritual connectedness. Ensuring that individuals with ASD are fully integrated into their faith community is not only

important to the individual and family but to the faith community. It provides the congregation with a true representation of the diversity of all
members of society and reflects a more accurate portrayal of individuals
living with disabilities. With the compassionate understanding and in-
creased knowledge found in THE CHILD WITH AUTISM LEARNS THE FAITH, we
are confident that faith communities will inflict fewer painful experiences
like the one Ms. Labosh shares in this book's opening pages.

This book's easy-to-use lessons and multisensory approach are just right
for teaching children with ASD. The practical tips will help congregations
engage all children with opportunities to grow in faith. The lessons can be
adjusted to accommodate for varying degrees of cognitive disabilities. The
contemplative questions for parents and caregivers are a wonderful guide
that can facilitate fellowship and help family members express underly-
ing sentiments that often-remain unspoken.

Ms. Labosh's initiative in developing this book is a testament to her own
dedication and commitment to the Christian faith. We commend her efforts to help faith communities incorporate all their members into the
full life of fellowship. THE CHILD WITH AUTISM LEARNS THE FAITH will in-
spire, encourage, and assist all those who share that priority. Statistics suggest ASD occurs in 1:166 children; surely this book is an essential tool for
every faith community that wants to provide meaningful participation to
all its members.

Sister Kathleen Schipani, IHM
Mrs. Lorie Brew
The Department for Pastoral Care for Persons with Disabilities
Archdiocese of Philadelphia

Preface
by Kathy Labosh

In 1994, my family visited a beautiful old cathedral while we were on vacation. Sam began babbling during the service and an usher came up and motioned for us to follow. I thought the usher would lead us to a cry room but instead we were escorted outside. The sound of those heavy doors closing behind us is unforgettable.

I knew God was not rejecting us — only the usher was — but the pain went deep nevertheless. Others might have left the church for good after an experience like that. Fortunately, it wasn't my home church and I loved God and my faith too much to leave.

I am very proud of my home diocese of Harrisburg. They started an out-reach group for families of children with developmental disabilities — St. Raphael's Outreach, named for the archangel whose name means "God Heals." At one meeting I listened to other parents talk about how hurt they felt when their children were turned down for religious education. The families felt isolated and abandoned by their church. My frustration and empathy turned into a sense of purpose — to get a religious education class started for the children in our church with developmental disabilities. My first step was to approach the director of religious education (DRE) about the need for a special education classroom. She said, "Great. I'll find you a room; just tell me what you need." I should have seen that coming, but I did not.

• • •

Courage is doing something scared, just because it needs to be done. I was terrified at the thought of this leading the religious education of the developmentally disabled, so I can empathize with DREs and teachers everywhere. Even with my knowledge of autism, I still felt overwhelmed. How scared and lost others must feel when they are dealing with an unfamiliar disability.

The class got started during the Christmas season, so my first class was called "Happy Birthday Jesus." I brought decorations, a cake, and small presents for the children. I realized in horror at the beginning of the class that I had forgotten the candles for the cake. As if on cue, someone from the church brought me a small candle with the picture of the nativity on the side as thank you gift for doing the class. It was the perfect candle for the cake! I felt God's blessing on my project and knew that He would make up for my weaknesses.

That first year was trying and exhilarating. There were days when I felt like a ringmaster in a circus gone awry. But even on those days, I saw God touching the children and the parents in unexpected ways. All God wanted from me was a willingness to reach out. We pray for God's help and we get it in abundance, because He wants our help in reaching these kids and families.

God will help you; He will be there for you as He was for me. He loves these children immensely. With this book you will be able to benefit from my experiences. Have courage and God bless.

—Kathy Labosh

. . .

Class Preparation
The Why, Who, When & What

Part one includes information
on the importance of developing ministry
targeted to the autistic population and
how to prepare for teaching them.
You will learn:

1

The Importance of Outreach

Many people are familiar with the parable of the ninety-nine sheep. The Good Shepherd has one hundred sheep and when he loses one, he leaves the other ninety-nine to go find the one that was lost. Well, I am going to tell you a parable of the stressed shepherd.

There once was a shepherd who had one hundred sheep. When one of them was missing, he knew it was the one with the black spot on his tail. He just wasn't like the other sheep. Sheep naturally follow other sheep; the stressed shepherd figured this one must be deaf and he must be a loner. He didn't seem to want to be near the other sheep.

So the next time the sheep with the black spot was missing, the stressed shepherd searched for a while and then returned to the flock. The shepherd had ninety-nine other sheep to tend. This one required more work than the other ninety-nine put together. It was not right to neglect them for this lamb who did not want to be a part of the flock anyway. This decision saddened the shepherd, but at the same time he felt a bit relieved.

Sometime later, a drought came upon the land. The shepherd's usual sources of water dried up. The sheep were struggling and so was he. The shepherd cried out to God for help and a fat sheep appeared on a hilltop. The shepherd followed the sheep into a box canyon where water was springing from a rock and vegetation was flourishing around the spring.

As the shepherd thanked God for saving him and his flock, he noticed that the fat sheep had a black spot on his tail. He wept when he realized that if he had taken the time to rescue that sheep, he would have found the spring before the drought had begun. He and his flock would have had a secret source of strength to see them through the drought.

The moral of the story is that we need every person to be complete. Those who bring the most challenges can draw the best out of us. When people see what someone with disabilities is up against, their own burden seems lighter. They resolve to try a little harder. Sick children draw more love, compassion, and patience out of us than a hundred sermons. They are God's powerful agents of change in the world today.

The families of children with developmental disabilities need the faith community around them, but there are many challenges. They are unable to bring their entire families to regular church functions because of their child's anxiety or behavior issues. They can feel judged by others who think autism is a discipline problem. Many marriages are tested by the strain. These families need to hear that God loves them, and that His people are here to support them. Unfortunately, their isolation makes them nearly invisible to those around them and they often suffer alone.

• • •

If your heart is ready to reach out to these families, this book will tell you how to accomplish that. You and your faith community will find blessings and strength that will carry you through the hardest times. Be encouraged by this scripture: "The learned will shine as brightly as the vault of heaven, and those who have instructed many in virtue as bright as stars for all eternity" (Daniel 12:3; Jerusalem Bible).

• • •

How They Learn

Before you can begin to teach a child with autism, you need to understand how autism affects the ability to process information. You will see why most traditional methods are inadequate to reach such children. More importantly you will learn simple teaching methods that do reach children with autism.

Autism is first and foremost a physical disability of the brain. The way blindness affects the eye or deafness affects the ear, autism affects the brain. Autopsies of people with autism have shown that some of their brain cells are small and immature as if they are waiting for some signal to develop. Other parts of the brain are over-developed. Furthermore, there are few of the thin filaments that connect one part of the brain to another. Although the problem is physical, the effects are often behavioral. So the first thing teachers and others who are working with the children must know is that autism is a disease that cannot be disciplined away. Teachers also must understand that children with autism have trouble processing information. Consider a typical children's book. It is full of intricate pictures, fanciful characters, and rich language meant to stimulate a child's imagination.

That is great for a typical child, but for a child with autism these features spell trouble. Those troubles can give you an insight into how the autistic mind works.

Intricate pictures work against children with autism. Everything on the page is treated equally in their eyes. No special importance is attached to any character or object. The number of bricks on the back wall may interest children with autism more than the characters in a story. Because they take in everything at once, they should be introduced slowly to a new environment and be allowed to explore. After they have mapped out everything in their head, whenever they enter a room they will only notice what is different. So, whether you're working with a picture from a book or an object in the room, you need to let your students with autism know which objects are significant to what you are teaching.

If you were reading a book out loud, they might have problems understanding you. They often have trouble distinguishing consonant sounds. CAT, BAT, MAT, FAT and RAT can sound fairly similar to them. To compensate for this deficiency, they tend to look at the speaker's mouth to lip read. Unfortunately, they then miss the expression in the speaker's eyes, which can transmit a lot of information. You need to speak slowly and enunciate clearly when you speak. Let your students see your face in case they need to lip read.

Individuals with autism would also have trouble understanding you if you were speaking in a noisy room. Typical people can focus in on one sound and filter out background noise; individuals with autism cannot. All noise is interpreted equally. The noisier the room, the less they will understand and the more agitated they will become. Cut down on background noise as much as possible, especially if the students are even a little bit stressed. You are teaching them important information; you want them to get it correctly.

Individuals with autism take everything literally. If there are fairies in a story, then fairies exist. They will not understand why you would tell them something that is not true. If you are telling them a fiction story than tell them it is "pretend" before you start. When you present stories from the Bible, stick to the story. Their simple faith is a beautiful gift. The parts of the brain that are involved in higher reasoning are physically impaired. Reasoning with individuals with autism is usually an exercise in frustration. Keep it simple or you risk losing credibility.

Watch what you teach and read to them. They will believe what you say — that is if they can understand you. Autism affects language comprehension. The biggest problem a child with autism faces when reading a book is the rich language. Single words are understood best, followed by simple sentences of two to three words. The higher the level of vocabulary and sentence structure, the less they will understand. Most religious education classes and regular classes are taught with textbooks and lectures. So, when children with autism are taught with other children, just about everything goes over their heads. They usually get in trouble by trying to occupy their time until the class ends. Just remember that the more you read and the more you speak, the less they understand.

All this may leave you wondering what methods of communication are left. Well, have you ever had a dream? In dreams, we think in pictures, and that is just what individuals with autism do. Most think in pictures instead of words. Individuals with autism process information about the world around them through physical interaction with it and by studying what they see. Thoughts run through their minds as a stream of images, like a videotape. They often communicate by bringing a person to what they want so the person can see it.

If you want to bring children with autism to knowledge of your faith, you need to use images as well as physical interaction with the objects they are studying. The lesson plans in this book are designed to reach the children this way. The spoken word is only used to supplement the pictures and other activities.

This may sound complicated, but it's not. In fact, it is an ancient way of passing on the faith. The walls of the catacombs of Rome are covered with pictures of Scripture stories. Even today if you look at the pictures, you know what stories were being told. Be encouraged. It is possible to bring these children to an understanding of the stories that have carried our faith across millennia.

● ● ●

Our forefathers fought many obstacles to bring faith to our generation. We need to join together to bring it to those with autism in the next generation. They deserve to be a part of the great sweep of religious history too.

● ● ●

The Classroom Setup

The ideal religious education or Sunday school class for children with autism would be led by a teacher experienced in special education and would include an aide for each child. There would be a separate table for each child and his aide to work on. The parents could be in a separate room getting a break from their kids and working on their own Bible study.

The problem is the dream classroom can be nearly impossible to set up and nightmarish to maintain. Special education professionals are often too tired from their regular jobs to want to lead another special education class. Teenagers make great aides until this sport or that activity interferes. You need a long list of volunteers. I have found that the best solution is to have the parents work with their child or another child. During that time, the parents can often discuss things that are going on in their lives and bond. It is easier to get an aide or two to fill in if needed than to get numerous aides to commit to months of classes. If things are different in your church or synagogue, I applaud your congregation.

Before the classes get started, it's important to meet with all of the parents. Each child's ability to comprehend language, their skill levels, and their behavior issues need to be discussed. You should also discuss goals for the year. Do the parents want their children to learn the Hebrew alphabet? Do they want their children to prepare for First Holy Communion? Are some of the parents simply interested in helping their children be more comfortable going into the church building? These goals can be worked on during "packet time," which we will discuss shortly.

Meeting with the parents will also help determine whether some children can be mainstreamed into a regular classroom with just a few minor adjustments. If a child can be mainstreamed, you and the parents should go over the regular lesson plan and highlight the facts that you want the child to know. Once those decisions are made, a series of fact cards can easily be made, tailored to that child's needs. Each fact should be divided onto two cards that the child must match to get the whole fact. For instance, "The two forms of the Eucharist" could be on one card and "bread and wine" would be on the other card. Make up several fact cards for the child. The child can work on matching facts while the other children are reading or listening to lectures. In this way, the mainstreamed child will receive the same information as the other children, only less of it. The mainstreamed child could have an aide to redirect his attention when necessary or to help him with any crafts. Keep in mind that fine motor skills are often difficult for children with autism.

For children who are too young for the religious education class, I suggest you make a social story for the kids about going to church or synagogue. Use photographs of the interior of your church or synagogue. You can turn the photos into flashcards that the parents can use for matching. In this way they can teach their children the names of the objects; they can also tell the social story of what goes on during a service. Parents can use this until their child is old enough to attend a class. (See page 107 for information on purchasing a social story kit.)

A child who does not have the cognitive or social skills necessary to be incorporated into a regular classroom is perfect for the disabilities class. These classes are structured to go through a series of individual and group activities. Each activity has a purpose but activities can be added or deleted to suit your situation. Not every activity is going to reach each child but everyone should be able to come away with something. Let's look at the order of activities and then we can take a closer look at some of them:

- Opening prayer (group)
- Circle time (group)
- Scripture reading (individually with aide)
- Packet time (individually with aide)
- Group activity (group)
- Video or music (group)
- Closing prayer (group)

The classes start with an opening prayer. This prayer should be an important one of your faith. Possible prayers could be the Our Father, Hail Mary, Modeh Ani, or Shema Yisrael. This prayer should be repeated at the start of every class. These children learn by repetition, and it won't be long before they start repeating the prayer with you.

Another purpose of the opening prayer is to announce the start of class. The children and their aides should gather for circle time. This talk should be short, related to the story, and pertinent to issues in their lives. I have provided circle time talks for each lesson.

After circle time, the children will go with their aide for scripture reading: Each child will read or be read to from an ability-appropriate Bible. These Bibles can range from a felt picture Bible to a study bible with photographs of the places and artifacts. A list of Bibles is included in Part One,Section D. After the Scripture reading is finished, the aide and child will work on individual activities found in their packet.

Packet time is the most important part of the class. Everyone is collectively taught one lesson, but each child has as aide (usually a parent) and individual work projects that match the skill and comprehension level of the child. These projects can include taking tours of the house of worship, matching pictures, doing puzzles, coloring pictures, reading books, making crafts, and learning Hebrew letters. Packet time is the time devoted to working on the yearly goal set for the child.

Group activity follows packet time, and it should be a fun activity for the kids that enables them to physically interact with the story in some fashion. Some kids will need a lot of help, others will not. Let the child choose his comfort level. Do not force the child to participate.

After the group activity, videos or songs can be played. This gives the adults a little time to share and clean up. It can also provide time for the parents to pursue a short Scripture study together. Part two provides lesson plans for the adults that correspond to the theme of the children's class.

Section D in Part One lists many thematically relevant story videos. Veggie Tales or other wholesome videos would be fine, too.

The kids love songs. If your congregation has musicians willing to share their talents with the children, they would find a very receptive audience.

13

Of course, you can also play CDs or a kids' music video. Some good options are listed in Part One, Section D.

The class ends with a closing prayer, which sums up a response to what the children have learned about God through that lesson. The closing prayer also signals to the children that the class is over.

This class is designed to be flexible. Feel free to add or delete sections to fit your needs and your time constraints. The parents' Scripture study, which accompanies each lesson, is optional but highly recommended. Parenting children with autism can feel isolating. It is good for parents to meet with others and find out they are not alone in their experiences. The Scripture study and discussion time provides an opportunity for a life-giving community to form.

Parents should do their reading ahead of class, but just reading the selected scripture with a general knowledge of the story is sufficient for discussion. Parents should come prepared to discuss the questions. They can do that while their kids are watching the video or just among themselves while working with kids. If they choose the latter option, parents should be careful when discussing any of the negative aspects of dealing with autism. Sometimes these kids understand more than you think.

● ● ●

This class is designed to meet the needs of children with autism **and** their parents. Most importantly, it is designed to pass faith on from one generation to the next in a way that meets the special needs of this population. Before you get started, the idea may feel like a massive undertaking, but it truly is not. Once you start working with the lessons, you will discover that you **can** do what God has asked you. Best yet, the kids will learn that they are an important and valuable part of your faith community.

● ● ●

The Materials

The best place to find materials is in your own congregation. They have books, videos, toys, and puzzles lurking in their basements, attics, and playrooms. They do not want to keep them, but they do not want to throw them out either. People want their things to go to good use. Giving it to special needs kids is a blessing for them and for you.

Of course, a wealth of new publications, videos, and toys are available in bookstores and on the Internet. In this chapter, I will introduce you to some of these products. You will find the information in the class segment where it will be used.

MATERIALS NEEDED FOR CIRCLE TIME AND GROUP PROJECTS

A complete list of materials needed is included with each lesson in Part Two . The list here provides an overall picture of items that will probably need to be purchased or borrowed. You can use this list to ask your congregation to pitch in. Items that you are likely to have around the house or yard (for instance, a flashlight or some rocks) or that can be easily and inexpensively purchased (fruit, crepe paper) are not included in this list.

- Terrarium kit (lesson 1)
- A variety of small stuffed animals (lessons 2 and 3)
- Baby name book (lesson 3)
- Noah's Ark toy (lesson 6)
- Striped, multi-colored robe (lesson 10)
- Cloth tunnels (lesson 11)
- Large cardboard boxes (lesson 11)
- Plastic eggs (lesson 12)
- Finger puppets of the ten plagues — available from www.oytoys.com (lesson 14)
- Certificates and awards (lesson 15)

SCRIPTURE READING

Bibles for the children should be based on their abilities. Basically any Bible the child enjoys is fine, but there are some that I particularly like. For a child who is non-verbal or with very limited language I recommend THE BEGINNER'S BIBLE, BIBLE BEGINNINGS-BOOK 1. This felt Bible is produced by Little Folk Visuals. It covers most but not all of the stories in this Bible study. The other stories can be covered by buying additional felt pieces. Little Folk Visuals also publishes a BIBLE IN FELT TEACHER'S MANUAL (Copyright 1966, revised 1992).

For the child with some language, I recommend EVERYDAY BIBLE STORIES by Our Sunday Visitor, illustrated by Anna C. Lepler. This book is wonderful because the stories are short and fill only one page. There are 365 stories, which take you all the way through the Bible. You can always read more than one page if you want to. The only downside is that the pages have a date at the top, which probably will not correspond to the day you are reading it. That feature will bother some children with autism.

For the older student, who does not want anything childish, I love THE CHILDREN'S ILLUSTRATED BIBLE stories retold by Selina Hasting, illustrated by Eric Thomas (DK Publishing, Inc., copyright 1994). It has fantastic photographs of the area as well as maps and pictures of artifacts. It still presents the story visually, but respects the student's age and maturity. The language level is okay too, especially with the photos.

DK Publishing also puts out A FIRST BOOK OF JEWISH BIBLE STORIES. I have not seen it, so I am not sure that it covers all of the stories that this lesson plan does.

Many of the children may already have a Bible appropriate to their abilities. This is something that should be ascertained during the meeting with the parents before the classes start.

For the parents' Scripture study I think that a variety of Bible versions can add to the Bible study. But whatever Bible people already have is surely sufficient. We do not want the classes to become burdensome in any way to the families by requiring things that are not truly needed.

PACKET TIME

Packets must be developed that are appropriate to each child's abilities and goals. A packet should be assembled for each child to work with individually with their aide. The work can mirror skills that they are currently working on in school or have already mastered. It is not difficult to put the packets together. Once you have the contents set, it is often just a case of updating the coloring picture and rotating the puzzles for each new lesson.

A low-functioning child may simply be matching pictures of animals, fruit, holy cards, or pictures of objects in your church. Their packets can also include coloring pages related to the story. Simple puzzles are another good option. Listening to their aide read stories is another possibility for packet time.

A more advanced child may be doing connect-the-dot puzzles and other higher-level puzzles, reading stories, and playing card games.

A child who uses sign language could be learning Bible verses in sign. A Jewish child could be learning his Aleph Bet. A Catholic child could be preparing for his First Holy Communion.

There are some great websites and catalogs that have a wonderful selection of children's toys and activities. Many of these are also available in local religious bookstores. The following list is just a launching point to give you an idea of what is out there and where you might find it. Once you start looking, you won't believe the variety of what's available.

- www.oytoys.com — For all things Jewish! Get puzzles and other activities to teach children the Aleph Bet. Also of interest of all at this website are:
  - TASTY BIBLE STORIES — A menu of tales and matching recipes by Tami Lehman-Wilzig, illustrated by Katherine Janus Kahn (Kar-Ben Publishing; 2003).
  - BIBLE STORY CRAFTS FOR LITTLE HANDS by Ruth Esrig Brinn, illustrated by Sally Springer (Kar-Ben Publishing; 2000). I particularly liked the Rachel's bracelets.
  - IN THE BEGINNING — A cloth activity book.
  - Creation Floor Puzzle (27 pieces)
  - Noah's Ark Floor Puzzle (24 Pieces)
  - Noah's Ark Shape Sorter
  - S.S. Noah Soft Playset
  - Noah's Ark Animal Match
  - Noah's Ark Sticker Stories
  - Passover Ten Plagues Finger Puppets — (lesson 14)

- The Autom Catalog at www.autom.com has a variety of books to prepare children to receive the sacraments. Items of more general interest at this website are:
  - Fun with Bible Friends Coloring Book
  - Bible Heroes Coloring Book
  - Noah and the Flood Puzzle Book by St. Joseph Puzzle Books. It has five 12-piece puzzles that correspond to the story on the opposite page.
  - Religious Fun and Game Book (assorted in pack - will contain Old and New Testament games)
  - Bible Bingo Game (mixture of Old and New Testament symbols)
  - The Hi God CD collection

- Various children's Bibles

- Pauline Books and Media at www.pauline.org carries:
  - THE BIBLE FOR LITTLE ONES translated by Mary Nazarene Prestofillipo FSP. This is a board book.
  - THE STORY OF NOAH'S ARK translated by Mary Nazarene Prestofillipo FSP. This is a board book.
  - Bible Stories — Find-the-Picture Puzzles

- Sadlier at www.sadlier.com has some wonderful large books that are terrific if you want to read in front of the children.
  - THE PRE-PRIMARY 1 — includes Abraham, Moses, Samuel, David and Goliath
  - THE PRE-PRIMARY 2 — includes Daniel, Jonah, Zacchaeus, the Little Lost Sheep
  - THE PRIMARY 1 — includes Elijah and the Big Showdown, Esther, Ruth, Joseph: The Favorite Son
  - THE PRIMARY 2 — includes Jesus Is with Us, Jesus' Miracles, Paul and Silas Go to Jail, Saul's Surprise on the Road to Damascus
  - Sadlier also carries a Bible Felt Art Kit, Pre K - 3

- Carson-Dellosa Publishing at www.carsondellosa.com
  - Bible Story Puppets and Poems
  - Interactive Bible Story Bulletin Boards
  - Easy Christian Crafts
  - Play and Learn Bible Games
  - The Good Book Cookbook
  - Signs of Wisdom — Expressing God's Wisdom in Sign Language
  - Faith Speaks — Expressing God's Word in Sign Language

- Name that Bible Character! — Puzzles and Clues from the Greatest Stories Ever Told
- Dot-to-Dot Bible Pictures
- Hidden Pictures
- Bible Story Puzzles

- Harcourt Religion Publishers at www.harcourtreligion.com
  - The Bible Big Books including ABRAHAM, GOD MADE OUR WORLD, JOSEPH: THE FAVORITE SON, MOSES, and NOAH. These may be purchased separately instead of in sets.
  - PRAY & PLAY BIBLE FOR YOUNG CHILDREN
  - PRAY & PLAY BIBLE 2 FOR YOUNG CHILDREN
  - Pray and Play Songs for Young Children

- Catholic Child at www.catholicchild.com
  - TOUCH AND FEEL BIBLE STORIES
  - LIFT THE FLAP CATHOLIC BIBLE
  - LIFT AND LOOK CREATION and Noah's Ark book set
  - NOAH'S ANIMAL ALPHABET PUZZLE
  - LIFT AND LEARN OLD TESTAMENT STORIES
  - Noah's Ark Playmobil Set
  - Noah's Rainbow Race Game
  - CDs and DVDs for children

- Standard Publishing at www.standardpub.com
  - Thru-the-Bible Reproducible coloring book, illustrated by Janet Skiles. This is good for all the lessons.
  - Bible Memory Game

- Cook Communication Ministries of Canada at www.cook.ca carries some of my favorites:
  - Bible Bingo
  - Bible Old Man (plays like Old Maid using Bible characters)
  - Jonah, Go Fish Card Game
  - Noah's Memory Match Up
  - Bible Dominoes
  - Who Do You See? Game (Plays like Where's Waldo)

- www.christianbook.com — more resources than you'll ever need are available from this Internet retailer.

VIDEOS AND SONGS

Videos

Finding quality videos and DVDs for teenagers can be tricky. You definitely want to stay away from the cute cartoons. They want to be treated with respect in regard to their age. I recommend The Bible Collection series put out by Turner Home Entertainment. They use famous actors and are generally very good. The video on Creation may be a little boring for the kids and hard to follow. The other videos in the series are great, just take Genesis a little at a time. The series covers: Genesis, Abraham, Jacob, Joseph, Moses, Samson and Delilah, David, Solomon, Esther, Paul the Apostle, and the Apocalypse.

The Bible in Animation series is good for elementary school kids. The series covers: Creation & the Flood, Abraham, Joseph, Moses, Ruth, David & Saul, Elijah, Daniel and Jonah.

For young children there are so many options: Veggie Tales, the Cherub Wings, the Wemmicks, and countless others.

You can find these videos and more at www.catholicvideo.com; www.christiancinema.com and www.christianbook.com.

Songs

Children with autism remember words that they hear in song better than those spoken to them. If you can incorporate songs into your program, it could be very beneficial. Here is a list of common songs (without copyright restrictions) that you may wish to incorporate:

- Adam was a Gardener
- Father Abraham
- Hava Nagila
- He's Got the Whole World in His Hands
- If You Are Happy and You Know It
- Jesus Loves Me
- Rise and Shine (The Arky, Arky Song)
- This Little Light of Mine

The words and tunes to these and other songs can be found at www.kididdles.com.

Numerous collections of worship songs and faith songs are available on CD from Internet retailers and your local religious bookstore. Probably some members of your congregation will have some they are willing to share or donate.

• • •

The fifteen lessons included in this book require a variety of materials, but many are durable materials that can be used again and again. Videos, CDs, Bibles, and toys can serve through many terms. Don't forget: people want to help out by supplying resources. Ask the congregation. Much of what you need, you will find right there. Look for reproducibles to include in the packets as well as durable puzzles and card games that can be rotated among the children's packets throughout the term.

• • •

Part Two

Faith Lessons for the Child with Autism

This section includes fifteen Bible lessons for children. Each lesson features specific directions for circle time and a group activity. Furthermore, each lesson is accompanied by a Scripture study for the parents. Specific instructions regarding ability-appropriate Bibles and preparing packets for packet time are included in Section D of Part One.

1

Creation:
God Made Everything

CHILDREN'S CLASS

Materials and Preparation

- Flashlight
- Water
- Rocks
- Plant
- A piece of fruit
- Stuffed animals
- A doll
- Terrarium kit(s)

You will need the flashlight, water, rocks, dirt, plants, a piece of fruit, stuffed animals and a doll for the children's circle time. Some of these items can be re-used during the group project if you opt to do the terrarium project. For the terrarium project, you can buy a plastic terrarium at a pet store as well as dirt and plants and other material to add to it. If someone has a small pet they would like to lend to the project, the animal can be added last to represent the animals God made (Note: Rabbits for some unknown reason have been known to terrify some children.)

Packets for the individual packet work should be prepared before the semester begins, according to the goals set for the individual students. Make sure packets are ready for each child before the first class. Choose an appropriate video or CD to use during the lesson.

Lesson Objective
To help the children understand that God made everything in nature.

Opening Prayer
The same opening prayer is prayed at the start of every lesson.

Circle Time
Look around you and you see lots of things. But once there was a time when there was absolutely nothing except God. Do you know what the first thing He made was? Light (Turn on the flashlight) Yup. Light! I guess He wanted to see. But He didn't make a flashlight. Man made that. God did make the sun and all the stars at night. Then He made the water. (Hold up the glass.) Then He made the earth that we are standing on. (Hold up the rock.) God made this. Next He made plants so that it would look beautiful (hold up plant) and there would be food for his creatures to eat (hold up fruit) and air for them to breathe. He then made all the birds, fish, and animals. (Hold up stuffed animals.)

God loved all the things He had made, but He wanted one more thing:

someone to love. So He made people (hold up doll). He called the first man Adam.

Scripture Reading

Each aide should read the creation story to their student from an ability-appropriate Bible.

Packet Work

Time to work individually (with their aide) on the goal-oriented work provided in the packet.

Group Activity

Use the terrarium kit to have the children make their own world by putting in dirt, rocks, and plants. Add water if plants are real.

Video/Songs

Choose a thematically appropriate video or selection of songs to play. During this time, the parents can meet for their Scripture study.

Closing Prayer

God, thank you for the air I breathe and the food I eat. Thank you for making me.

PARENTS' SCRIPTURE STUDY

Individual Reading

Read Genesis 1:1-2:4

Selected Scripture

"In the beginning, when God created the heavens and the earth, the earth was a formless wasteland, and darkness covered the abyss, while a mighty wind swept over the waters.

Then God said, 'Let there be light,' and there was light. God saw how good the light was. God then separated the light from the darkness. God called the light 'day' and darkness he called 'night'. Thus evening came and morning followed — the first day." (Genesis 1:1-5).

Contemplation

When most people want to explain the creation story and the wonders of God to children, they usually start with all the wonderful plants and animals He created. However, the first thing God created was order, a schedule we can plan our lives around.

Children with autism crave order and schedules. One way of introducing the awesome power of God to a child might be to set up God's schedule for the day. Find out what times the sun and moon will rise and set. Learn when the moon will be full and the tides high. Show them that God made a schedule that the world and the universe follow.

Discussion Questions:

1. How does God's creation speak to you?

2. Is there a way you can share that experience with your child?

3. How might God's creation speak most powerfully to your child?

Adam Names the Animals: God Has a Job for Us

Materials and Preparation

- Several small stuffed animals
- Index cards with animal names written on them to match the stuffed animals

You will need a variety of small stuffed animals for the children to name. These will be used later for the zoo.

Rotate packet items and add new items as necessary. Choose an appropriate video or CD to use during the lesson.

Lesson Objective

To teach the children that God has a job for them, just as he has a job for every person.

Opening Prayer

The same opening prayer is prayed at the start of every class.

Circle Time

After God made Adam, He gave Adam a job to do. He wanted Adam to give a name to all the animals. Adam saw everything that God made and really liked it. It was a big job coming up with all those names and remembering them too. He worked hard and was proud of the all those names.

God has a job for everybody. One of our jobs is to learn about God and to learn about his world. God is very happy when we work hard at these jobs.

Scripture Reading

Each aide should read the story of Adam naming the animals to their student from an ability-appropriate Bible.

Packet Work

Time to work individually (with their aide) on the goal-oriented work provided in the packet.

Group Activity

Make a zoo. There should be small stuffed animals or animal figurines around the room. Each child should have a few cards with the name of an animal on it. With their aide, each child should put the appropriate card beside the animals. When everyone is done, the class can take a tour of the zoo.

Video/Songs

Choose a thematically appropriate video or selection of songs to play. During this time, the parents can meet for their Scripture study.

Closing Prayer
God help me do my job. Help me to learn about you and your world.

Note
Tell the parents to bring photos of family and friends next week.

PARENTS' SCRIPTURE STUDY

Individual Reading
Read Genesis 2:4-20

Selected Scriptures
"The Lord God then took the man and settled him in the Garden of Eden, to cultivate and care for it" (Genesis 2:15).

"So the Lord God formed out of the ground various wild animals and various birds of the air, and brought them to the man to see what he would call them; whatever the man called each of them would be its name" (Genesis 2:19).

Contemplation
Even in the Garden of Eden, God had a job for man to do. People whose jobs have meaning and purpose have a contented heart and a joy that others lack. The job does not have to be a religious one; an individual's calling can be to be a doctor, a trash collector, or an administrative assistant. It is whatever we were made for. God has jobs for us to do. Those jobs are not just about lifetime careers. The jobs can be found in everyday life.

Our children have a purpose too. Nicky, my nine-year-old son, is non-verbal, but he is the refiner of my soul. He has taught me more about patience, unconditional love, humility, and the redemptive side of suffering than any theologian ever could. So often as parents our capacity to love exceeds what we ever dreamed possible because of our children. Children challenge and transform the people around them to become better people. If that is not doing God's work, what is?

Discussion Questions

1. Has your life found a new purpose since autism entered your family?

2. How has having a child with autism affected your own spiritual development?

3. What do you think God's plan for your child is for today and in the future?

• • •

Adam & Eve:
God Made Us for Others

CHILDREN'S CLASS

Materials and Preparation

- Pictures of family and friends
- A large picture of a tree with Adam and Eve at the bottom
- Baby names book for parents' study

Rotate and add packet items as necessary. Choose an appropriate video or CD to use during the lesson.

Lesson Objective
To teach the children that we are all part of God's family.

Opening Prayer
The same opening prayer is prayed at the start of every lesson.

Circle Time

Adam looked all around and saw all the wonderful things that God had made and he worked very hard at naming everything. Adam loved everything that God made and thought God had done a good job. But there was one problem — Adam was lonely. He wanted someone like him to love and to share these things with. God understood, so God made a woman for Adam. He was so excited to have a friend, someone he could talk to and love. Adam named her Eve. Together, they made man's first creation: a family.

We are made to be a part of families or groups of friends. We are all different but we were made to love each other. Just like God loves us.

Scripture Reading

Using an ability-appropriate Bible, each aide should read the story of Adam and Eve to their student.

Packet Work

Time to work individually (with their aide) on the goal-oriented work provided in the packet.

Group Activity

Make a family and friends tree. Have the kids come up and place their photos on a group tree, which has Adam and Eve at the bottom. After everyone's photos have been added, take a picture of it. Then let the students take their photos back to make their own tree to take home.

Video/Songs

Choose a thematically appropriate video or selection of songs to play. During this time, the parents can meet for their Scripture study.

Closing Prayer

God, thank you for the friends and family that you have given me.

PARENTS' SCRIPTURE STUDY

Individual Reading

Read Genesis 2:20-25 and 3:20.

Selected Scripture

"The man called his wife Eve, because she became the mother of all the living" (Genesis 3:20)

Contemplation

In Scripture, names play a very important role. They not only identify the person, but they often speak of their role in God's plan. Parents in biblical times often used the names of their children as a form of prayer to God. And God sometimes changed people's names at a momentous time in their life. Abram became Abraham and Sarai became Sarah. In the book of Ruth, Naomi changed her own name to Marah, which means bitter. She wanted the world to know her sorrow over losing three sons.

I named my sons Samuel (of God) Mark (Hammer) and Nicholas (People of Victory) David (Beloved). I believe their names reflect their roles. In early times, hammers were used to shape metal into useful objects. My experience with my sons has transformed me into someone who can help bring others to victory in their lives. I owe it to God, my sons, and pure (Kathryn) grace (Anne) — which is what my name means.

Discussion Questions

1. What does your child's name mean?

2. Is there a particular reason that you picked that name?

3. Can you see God's plan in that name?

4. What does your name mean?

5. If you could rename yourself, what would your name mean?

● ● ●

Temptation:
Sin Hurts but God Always Loves Us

Materials and Preparation

- Different kinds of fruit
- Individual bowls for the children
- Plastic spoons

For the group project, get bowls for the children to choose their own fruit for a fruit salad. Do not mix the fruit ahead of time. They can be picky eaters and may want all their fruit separate.

Rotate and add packet items as needed. Choose an appropriate video or CD to use during the lesson.

Lesson Objective

To help the children understand that sin is God's name for things that hurt us.

Opening Prayer

The same opening prayer is prayed at the start of every lesson.

Circle Time

Sometimes children do naughty things, like running into the street. even though parents and teachers tell us not to do that. Why is that dangerous? Well, if a car hits you, you could get very hurt and your parents and teachers want to keep you well. If you get hit by a car, your parents will still love you. but you will have to work very hard to get well again.

God tells us all what to do and what not to do too. The things we do that can really hurt us or others He calls sin. If we sin, we can hurt in many different ways. God will still love us, but He will have to work with us to get us back to being good.

God gave Adam and Eve all sorts of good fruit to eat in the Garden of Eden, but He told them there was one fruit that would be bad for them. Adam and Eve ate that bad fruit anyway. God was sad because Adam and Eve could not live in Eden anymore. Adam and Eve sinned, but God still loved them.

Scripture Reading

Using an ability-appropriate Bible, each aide should read the story of Adam and Eve's sin to their student.

Packet Work

Time to work individually (with their aide) on the goal-oriented work provided in the packet.

Group Activity
Make a fruit salad.

Set out bowls of fruit and have the kids make their own fruit salad in their own bowl. Some children may only want one kind of fruit in their fruit "salad." Make a fruit salad with all the remaining fruit for the parents who are not as picky about what they eat. Say a prayer thanking God for all the good fruit He provides and the farmers who raise it.

Video/Songs
Choose a thematically appropriate video or selection of songs to play. During this time, the parents can meet for their Scripture study.

Closing Prayer
God help me to tell when I have been naughty. Help me to do better and keep trying.

PARENTS' SCRIPTURE STUDY

Individual Reading
Read Genesis 3

Selected Scriptures
"Then he asked, 'Who told you that you were naked? You have eaten, then, from the tree of which I had forbidden you to eat!' The man replied, 'The woman whom you put here with me — she gave me fruit from the tree, and so I ate it.' The Lord God then asked the woman, 'Why did you do such a thing?' The woman answered, 'The serpent tricked me into it, so I ate it'" (Genesis 3:11-13).

Contemplation

When things go wrong it is human nature to look for someone to blame. We blame ourselves, others, God, or the devil. When it comes to autism, many parents carry a large burden of guilt. Others blame the environment or vaccines. If someone or something was at fault, then we believe that it was controllable.

We believe in the myth that we control what happens to us. To an extent we do control what happens to us because our actions do have consequences. But there is much we cannot control. We cannot control what other people do. We could not control when and where we were born. We could not control who our family was. Most of us cannot even control how much we eat. How reasonable is it to believe we could have controlled whether our child got autism? Many of us would rather feel guilty than out of control.

In the Bible we see bad things do happen to good people. Sin entered here and will continue to wreak havoc. But we also see God enter into each of those situations and make it work for the good. We cannot control what happens to us. God does not force others to do what He wants anymore than He forces us. But He can make any situation work out for our ultimate good.

We cannot know or control the future or change the past. There is no cause for insecurity, because God will be there and was there. Most importantly, He is here now, making everything work out for our good. Free yourself from anxiety and forgive yourself and others. Embrace this and you will find peace.

Discussion Questions

1. Do you blame yourself for your child's condition?

2. Do you blame your spouse?

3. Who or what is your anger directed at?

4. Does blame or anger make your situation any better?

• • •

Cain & Abel

Hurting Others Makes Things Worse

CHILDREN'S CLASS

Materials and Preparation

- Food treats - donuts, cookies, and so forth
- Small toys — small balls, Slinkies, Playdoh, and Happy Meal toys. Make sure you have plenty of duplicates in case several children want the same thing.

I don't recommend using some of the snacks from the group project snack tray during the circle time talk. The kids' attention will be focused on the snack and they will want it right away. For the group activity, the children will practice asking by word or sign for what they want.

Rotate or add packet items as needed.
Choose an appropriate video or selection of songs to play.

Lesson Objective

To teach the children that asking for what you want is better than stealing or being angry.

Opening Prayer

The same opening prayer is prayed at the start of every lesson.

Circle Time

Did you ever want a cookie that someone else had? If you grabbed the cookie, I'll bet you get a lot more than the cookie. You get everyone mad at you too. And I'll bet you didn't even get the cookie. It probably got taken away from you. Grabbing probably made everything worse.

What should you do when you want a cookie that someone else has? You can ask your parents or teacher if you can have a cookie too. Did you know that we can ask God for the things we want or need? Sometimes He says, "Yes," and sometimes He says, "No," and sometimes He says, "Later." The best times are when He says, "I have something better for you." If we learn to do things God's way, everyone is better off. Cain was mad at his brother Abel because He thought God liked Abel more. Cain did not ask God what he could do to make God happy. Cain got mad instead. Let's read to see what happened.

Scripture Reading

Using an ability-appropriate Bible, each aide should read to their student the story of Cain and Abel.

Packet Work

Time to work individually (with their aide) on the goal-oriented work provided in the packet.

Group Activity

This is a project to help the children learn to ask for what they want.

Have several treats or toys on a big plate. Have the kids ask for what they want through sign, pictures, or words. If they are able, have them ask God for what they want. Write those requests down and have them pray, "God help." When we did this group project, my son asked for a white donut. Believe me, he got it.

Video/Songs

Choose a video or selection of songs to play. During this time, the parents can meet for their Scripture study.

Closing Prayer

God, help me to ask you for what I need. Help me to share what I have.

Parents' Scripture Study

Individual Reading

Read Genesis 4:1-6

Selected Scripture

"...The Lord looked with favor on Abel and his offering but on Cain and his offering He did not. Cain greatly resented this and was crestfallen" (Genesis 4:4-5)

Contemplation

It is hard for me when I encounter young children who are talking so effortlessly. I wonder how they can do that. My ten-year-old son still cannot talk. My thirteen-year-old has major issues with language. I grieve for my kids and for myself. It seems like life is not fair.

Cain felt life was not fair too. He had a home, a good job farming the land, and a close relationship with God where he could talk to him directly. He counted these blessings as nothing because he did not have the favor that God placed on Abel's sacrifices. After Cain killed Abel, he lost all those blessings that he had taken for granted and he wept. To make matters worse, Cain did not gain the favor in God's eyes that he had coveted.

When we look at the blessings that other people have, we can lose sight of what we do have. We lose the enjoyment we could be getting from them.

When you envy others, you might as well have nothing because that is the value you place on everything that is yours.

Discussion Questions

1.   What blessings do you have in your life?

2.   Do you view your child's autism as a punishment from God?

3.   Do you think God loves others more because their children are healthy?

4.   Is your child with autism a blessing?

● ● ●

6

Noah:
God Finds a Way to Save Us

CHILDREN'S CLASS

Materials and Preparation

- Noah's Ark toy
- Some extra matching pairs of animals (as necessary) to provide at least one set for each student

The Noah's Ark toy should be used for display during circle time. The same one is used later in the group project. For the group project each child will be given several pairs of animals to match and put on the ark.

Rotate and add packet items as necessary. Choose an appropriate video or CD to use during the lesson.

Lesson Objective
To reassure the children that God is with us during times of change.

50

Opening Prayer

The same opening prayer is prayed at the start of every lesson.

Circle Time

Sometimes things change and it can be upsetting. Sometimes we might have to move or go to a new class. We are afraid because we do not know what will happen. But God is with us where we are now, He is with us when we are going through the changes, and He will be there in the new place. God finds a way to keep us safe with Him. Noah was a man who encountered big scary changes. We'll hear about that when we all do our Bible reading.

Scripture Reading

Using an ability-appropriate Bible, each aide should read the story of Noah to their student.

Packet Time

Time to work individually (with their aide) on the goal-oriented work provided in the packet.

Group Activity

Provide each student with some matching animals to put on Noah's Ark. Students should take turns bringing their pair of animals to the ark.

Video/Songs

Choose a thematically appropriate video or selection of songs to play. During this time, the parents can meet for their Scripture study.

Closing Prayer

God, thank you for saving us when we are in trouble. Help us when we need to change.

PARENTS' SCRIPTURE STUDY

Individual Reading

Read Genesis chapters 6 and 7

Selected Scripture

"In the six hundredth year of Noah's life, in the second month, on the seventeenth day of the month: it was on that day that 'All the fountains of the great abyss burst forth, and the floodgates of the sky were opened.' For forty days and forty nights, heavy rain poured down on the earth" (Genesis 7:11).

Contemplation

Do you remember the day you first heard the word **autism** in regard to your child? For most parents, that day starts the deluge. The days become a blur of worry, tears, and trying to find a cure. After a while, you get your feet underneath you again, but you find yourself in a whole new world. Everything has changed.

God is the ark that carries us through these changes. God's people are not spared the circumstances that affect others. We may be rocked and uncertain about the future, but we are able to endure. Later we are able to overcome and build a new world for our families and others.

Discussion Questions

1. What do you remember about the experience of learning that your child has autism?

2. Are you still in the middle of the storm or are your feet on solid ground?

3. How has your world changed since autism entered your life?

4. Where has God been in this process?

• • •

Abraham:
God Starts Many Nations

CHILDREN'S CLASS

Materials and Preparation

You can get the tune for the "Father Abraham" song at www.kididdles.com and in many songbooks. The words have been changed to accommodate the abilities and sensitivities of the children with autism.

Rotate and add packet items as needed. Choose an appropriate video or CD to use during the lesson.

Lesson Objective

To show the children that God can do great things with a person who loves Him.

Opening Prayer

The same opening prayer is prayed at the start of every lesson.

Circle Time

Sometimes one man can have many children. Those children then have children and it goes on and on through the years. That first father is called a patriarch. A patriarch of our faith is the first person to believe in God the way we do. Abraham is the father of many peoples and faiths. He had two sons: Isaac and Ishmael. Isaac is the father of all the Jewish people and Ishmael became the father of many Arab people. Christianity was started by Jesus, a descendent of Abraham, so Christians call Abraham their father in faith.

You never know what great things God can do with one person who loves Him and follows Him. God can do great things with you too, just like He did with Abraham.

Scripture Reading

Using an ability-appropriate Bible, each aide should read to their student the story of Abraham.

Packet Work

Time to work individually (with their aide) on the goal-oriented work provided in the packet.

Group Activity

Gather the children together, in a circle if possible. This little song is to the tune of "Father Abraham." The original calls for the children to make arm and leg movements, which would be difficult for many of the kids. I have also made it more personal for the children by incorporating their names.

"Father Abraham had many kids.
Many kids had Father Abraham.
I am one of them, so is (child's name)
So let's just praise the Lord.
AMEN!"

(Repeat for each child.)

Video/Songs

Choose a thematically appropriate video or selection of songs to play. During this time, the parents can meet for their Scripture study.

Closing Prayer

God, do great things with my life. I pray that what I do would bring glory and honor to you.

Parents' Scripture Study

Individual Reading

Read Genesis 16, 17, 21:1-21 and 24

Selected Scripture

"Sarah noticed the son whom Hagar the Egyptian had borne to Abraham playing with her son Isaac, so she demanded of Abraham: 'Drive out that slave and her son. No son of that slave is going to share the inheritance with my son Isaac.' Abraham was greatly distressed, especially on account of his son Ishmael. But God said to Abraham: 'Do not be distressed about the boy or about your slave woman. Heed the demands of Sarah, no matter what she is asking of you; for it is through

Isaac that descendents shall bear your name. As for the son of the slave woman, I will make a great nation of him also, since he too is your offspring'" (Genesis 21:9-13).

Contemplation

Have you ever wished you could go back into the past and change a decision that you made? Sarah sure did. She did not have Abraham's faith that everything would work out the way God said. All she could see was her own inadequacy. She did not think that God could work through her, so she figured God would have to work through her servant. Sarah tried to make God's promise come true in her own way and it blew up in her face pretty quickly. She lived with it begrudgingly until she saw that God had an entirely different plan — one that involved her. God was going to do for her what she could not accomplish on her own. Then she tried to get rid of Ishmael. He was messing things up for her.

God again had other plans. He loved Ishmael. He was Abraham's son too. He promised to bless him and make a great nation out of him. God loves us whether our parents planned for us or not, whether our parents wanted us or not. In the Bible, we see that many great people were born under questionable or difficult circumstances.

The truth is if God did not use our stumbling and our poor efforts to follow Him, He would have nothing to work with. He can do great things with whatever we bring Him, but He can do marvelous things when we obey Him and have faith.

When I look upon all the stress that autism has brought into my life, I can wonder what life would have been like if my son Nicky had never been conceived. But when he is happy and full of giggles, I think of all the joy I would have missed out on. I see what Nicky has done for my character development. I am more patient, kind, and non-judgmental. I do not know if autism is caused by man's mistakes with the environment, but I do know that Nicky is a gift from God and that he was meant to be.

Discussion Questions

1. Do you ever wonder what life would be like if your child with autism had never been conceived?

2. What are some of the hardships that you face with your child? (Do not share this in front of the children)

3. What are some of the joys?

• • •

8

Isaac & Rebekah:
Choosing Good Friends

Children's Class

Materials and Preparation

Develop a short script to depict several situations where people are acting as friends or not as friends. You may want to include skits on cigarettes, drugs, and sexual abuse. Ask some of the aides to volunteer to perform the skits.

Rotate and add packet items as needed. Choose an appropriate video or CD to use during the lesson.

Lesson Objective

To teach the children that good friends help them and that people who hurt them are not friends.

Opening Prayer

The same opening prayer is prayed at the start of every lesson.

Circle Time

There are many people around us, some are good and some are not. How can we tell whether they would be a good friend or not? Abraham's servant was given a job to find a good wife for Isaac. He decided a good way to tell if someone was nice was to look at how they helped others. Not just how they help their friends but even how they help strangers and animals.

This **is** a good way to tell if someone would be a good friend. Do they help others? Do they say nice things about other people? A friend would never tell us to do something wrong or something that would hurt us. If someone tells you to do something wrong or dangerous, that person is not a friend!

The other thing Abraham's servant did was pray to God. He asked God to bring the right wife for Isaac to him. We need to pray that God send the right friends into our lives.

Scripture Reading

Using an ability-appropriate Bible, each aide should read the story of Isaac and Rebekah to their student.

Packet Work

Time to work individually (with their aide) on the goal-oriented work provided in the packet.

Group Activity

Parents or other adults should act out different situations and ask the kids whether that person is being a friend or not. Be sure to portray a few scenarios for people acting like friends and for those not acting like friends. Friends could help someone up or tell someone they are doing a good job. People who are not friends could offer someone else cigarettes or drugs or make fun of people. I strongly suggest that a skit about sexual abuse take place because our kids are particularly vulnerable.

Video/Songs

Choose a thematically appropriate video or selection of songs. During this time, parents can meet for their Scripture study.

Closing Prayer

God, give us friends who bring us closer to you. Protect us from people who want to hurt us and want us to do wrong.

PARENTS' SCRIPTURE STUDY

Individual Reading

Read Genesis 24

Selected Scripture

"While I stand here at the spring and the daughter of the townspeople are coming out to draw water, if I say to a girl 'Please lower your jug, that I may drink,' and she answers, 'Take a drink, and let me give water to your camels, too,' let her be the one whom you have decided upon for your servant Isaac..." Genesis 24:13-14

Contemplation

Watching how someone treats strangers and animals is a good test of character. How you treat someone who cannot repay you is a show of an unselfish and hospitable heart.

Many parents of children with autism are single because autism can put a tremendous strain on a marriage. If you are single and looking for a new relationship, then observing how someone treats your child with autism can be a real eye-opener into that person's heart.

Stress can bring out the worst in people or it can bring out the best. If you react negatively to stress you can be irritable, angry, and emotionally overwrought. Stress leads some people to try to self-medicate with food, alcohol, or drugs. These responses are certainly human. With God's help we can use these stresses to become kinder, less judgmental, more loving, and more patient. It is a long and difficult transformation process.

The best we can do is flawed, but flawed is okay. We cannot cure autism or change the minds of everyone around us, but we can love our child as he is.

Discussion Questions

1. How do you react to stress?

2. How does your spouse or ex-spouse react?

3. What are ways to relieve the stress on both of you?

4. Do your expectations of yourself or your spouse add to the stress?

9

Jacob:
The Trickster

CHILDREN'S CLASS

Materials and Preparation

- Poster board with picture of ladder
- Rungs to place on ladder
- Glue stick

For the group project draw a ladder on a large piece of posterboard. Write "God's Laws" on one side of the ladder and "God's Prophets" on the other side. Using construction paper, cut out several rungs for the students to place on the ladder. Each rung should be labeled with words like "Prayer," "Reading Scripture," "Reading God's Word," "Doing what God's says," and "Believing in God". Modify and create rungs that would be significant to your faith's beliefs and practices. You should have at least one rung per child.

Lesson Objective

To show the children that there are many ways to get closer to God.

Opening Prayer

The same opening prayer is prayed at the start of every lesson.

Circle Time

Did you ever hit somebody only to have them hit you back? It hurt, didn't it? Jacob had a twin brother — Esau. Jacob tricked his brother out of his birthright and his father's blessing. Esau was very mad. Jacob went away to visit his uncle Laban. Do you know what happened? Laban tricked Jacob into marrying both of his daughters. Now Jacob was mad. He learned how it feels to be tricked out of something you worked hard for. When Jacob went back home, he brought Esau lots of gifts and presents to make up for tricking him. Esau forgave Jacob. God blessed both Jacob and Esau.

When we hurt somebody, we need to say we are sorry and try to make things right. God taught Jacob a lesson and He teaches lessons to us too.

Scripture Reading

Using an ability-appropriate Bible, each aide should read the story of Jacob to their student.

Packet Work

Time to work individually (with their aide) on the goal-oriented work provided in the packet.

Group Activity

On his way to see Laban, Jacob had a wonderful dream. He dreamed of a ladder going up to God. Today we are going to build a ladder. We are going to put on it the steps that bring us closer to God.

A ladder has two sides that hold it up. On one side, we have written "God's Law" and on the other side "God's Prophets." God's law is found in Scripture where He tells us what to do. God's prophets are the people who tell us when we are not doing right.

(Have the children come forward one by one to add their rung to the ladder. Use a glue stick to add the rungs.)

Okay, now our ladder looks pretty good. But remember, a ladder cannot take you anywhere unless you climb it.

Video/Songs
Choose a thematically appropriate video or selection of songs. During this time, parents can meet for their Scripture study.

Closing Prayer
God, help me to believe and do good things.

PARENTS' SCRIPTURE STUDY

Individual Reading
Read Genesis 25:19 through Genesis 33

Selected Scripture
"So, Isaac settled in Gerar. When the men of the place asked about his wife, he answered, "She is my sister." He was afraid, if he called her

his wife, the men of the place would kill him on account of Rebekah, since she was very beautiful" (Genesis 26:7).

Contemplation

A woman I know sent out a Christmas card with her family dressed in Christmas sweaters. What only her family knew was that her son with autism was wearing only the sweater. They cropped the photo so that they would appear acceptable. When I heard this story, I thought it was very representative of the life of a family with autism.

As a mother of two boys with autism, I know how deep the desire is to be able to act like a typical family. Sometimes I am afraid of what people might think. Maybe they will think that I am a bad mother or, worse yet, abusing my child.

One night in a hotel room, my son became very agitated and started hitting his head and screaming. I knew what it must sound like on the other side of the wall. Fortunately, my son had gotten lost in the hotel earlier that day and the staff knew what he was like. The police or child services were never called.

Jacob had fears too. He was afraid to present his family the way it actually was. He also feared the very possible consequences. But he was not genuinely secure until the truth came out. Then the king was upset that Jacob had not told him about Rebekah.

I was secure in the hotel room, only because the nature of my son's disorder was known to others. Letting people into our lives can be painful, and it must be done with some discretion. But as a family, we cannot feel loved and accepted as we are until people know us as we are.

The place to start is with other families with autism. They are most likely to understand. I would be cautious about people who are rigid and "by the book." Our lives seem to be written between the lines or in the margins. Often we figure things out as we go.

Discussion Questions

1.   Are you afraid to let people see you and your family as you are?

2.   How do you feel when people pass judgment on you?

3.   Do you assume that people are thinking the worst?

4.   Who is the worst critic of your parenting? You or someone else?

. . .

Joseph and His Dreams: God Has a Plan for Us

Materials and Preparation

- Multi-colored striped robe
- Several roles of crepe paper in different colors

Rotate and add packets items as needed. Choose an appropriate video or CD to use during the lesson.

Lesson Objective

To help the children understand that God has a plan for every person's life.

Opening Prayer

The same opening prayer is prayed at the start of every lesson.

Circle Time

Joseph was one of Jacob's sons. Jacob loved Joseph very much. Jacob gave Joseph a very special coat of many colors. Joseph's brothers were mad because they did not get a coat like that.

God loved Joseph very much too. God gave Joseph special dreams. Those dreams told Joseph that God had a special plan for him. Joseph's brothers were mad because they did not get dreams like that.

Joseph's brothers did something very naughty. They sold Joseph as a slave to some people. The brothers thought this would stop God's plan. It did not. God had a plan for Joseph's brothers too. He just did not tell them about it in a dream. They would have to live their lives first to find out about the plan.

God has a plan for your life whether you know it or not. Just like Joseph and his brothers, it is for good and great things. If we love God and try to follow him, other people will not be able to stop it.

Scripture Reading

Using an ability-appropriate Bible, each aide should read the story of Joseph and his family life to their student.

Packet Work

Time to work individually (with their aide) on the goal-oriented work provided in the packet.

Group Activity

Use crepe paper to add colored stripes to everyone's clothes. Have as much fun as you want by circling people with the crepe paper. Do whatever the children find fun.

Video/Songs

Choose a thematically appropriate video or selection of songs. During this time, parents can meet for their Scripture study.

Closing Prayer

Thank you God for having a special plan for my life even if I do not know what it is now.

PARENTS' SCRIPTURE STUDY

Individual Reading

Read Genesis 37.

Selected Scripture

"When his brothers saw that their father loved him best of all his sons, they hated him so much that they would not even greet him" (Genesis 37:4)

Contemplation

It can hurt to be reminded of all you want and cannot have. His brothers wanted their father's love and approval and could not get it. When Joseph boasted of all the great things that were going to happen to him, it dug like a knife into his brothers' pain. They wanted to ignore his existence. Getting rid of Joseph would not win their father's approval, but they would not have to be reminded of it daily.

Hope can hurt. Sometimes when a new treatment or product comes along, you do not even want to hear about it. You've already been down that road, and every time it's ended in disappointment. So we try and kill that little voice inside us that wants to hope and just be reconciled to how life is.

Despair is hope thrown down a well. Sometimes we're hurting on the inside, but we don't allow ourselves to hear it or truly feel it. If we allow hope and despair to speak, we will find they are the same part of us. Sometimes we put our hope in this treatment or that treatment and when it fails we lose our hope in God. This can happen when we think we're sure about the way God is going to work something out.

If we truly pour out our hopes, fears, and disappointments to God until we feel heard, then we can feel peace. We can accept when things do not go our way without despairing. When we know God has heard our cry, we will know that He is at work.

Discussion Questions

1. Does it hurt to hope sometimes?

2. Do you ever feel like God has let you down?

3. Does it hurt you to see "typical" children?

4. Do you feel too ashamed of those feelings to tell God about them?

● ● ●

Joseph in Egypt:
God's Plan is a Challenge

Materials and Preparation

- Cloth tunnels
- Large cardboard boxes
- Treat

Set up an obstacle course for the kids to go through. You can use cloth tunnels or cut open cardboard boxes for them to climb through. Have a treat at the end for them.

Rotate and add packet items as needed. Choose an appropriate video or CD to use during the lesson.

Lesson Objective
To help the children understand that following God is not easy.

Opening Prayer

The same prayer is prayed at the start of every lesson.

Circle Time

Joseph had a really hard time in Egypt. Some people were very mean to him. They lied about him and even threw him in jail. God made sure that there were also nice people around to help him. God never stopped loving Joseph. He got Joseph out of jail and left him in charge of the whole country. Joseph's brothers came and they were very sorry for hurting Joseph. Joseph forgave his brothers and they were able to live as a family again.

Sometimes people do mean things to us. God sees that and someday he will bring things right. We need to look for the nice people to help us through the hard times. Turn over the bad people to God. Following God is hard and forgiving people is harder, but everyone benefits if we forgive.

Scripture Reading

Using an ability-appropriate Bible, each aide should read the story of Joseph in Egypt to their student.

Packet Work

Time to work individually (with their aide) on the goal-oriented work provided in the packet.

Group Activity

Set up an obstacle course for the kids to go through. You can have little cloth tunnels for them to crawl through, tables to crawl under, and chairs to climb over. At the end of the obstacle course, let there be a nice snack reward. Tell the kids that following God can be hard, but there is always a reward at the end.

Video/Songs

Choose a thematically appropriate video or selection of songs. During this time, parents can meet for their Scripture study.

Closing Prayer

God, help us to follow you and trust you even when life gets hard. Help us to forgive those who hurt us. Change their hearts so they can follow you, too.

PARENTS' SCRIPTURE STUDY

Individual Reading

Read Genesis chapter 39 through chapter 45.

Selected Scripture

"He seized Joseph and threw him into the jail where the royal prisoners were confined. But even while he was in prison, the Lord remained with Joseph; he showed him kindness by making the chief jailer well-disposed toward him" (Genesis 39:20-21).

Contemplation

Joseph reminds me of Job. Both were men who had horrible things happen to them. Job lost his family, his livelihood, his money, and his health. Joseph was betrayed by his family, sold into slavery, falsely accused, and thrown into prison. Both, according the Bible, were highly favored by God.

Many people think that if bad things happen to you, like your child getting autism, that you must have done something spiritually to deserve it. Job's friends thought that and told him so often. Sometimes we tell ourselves that. The selected Scripture shows that God was with Joseph in his troubles, trying to make his life a little easier.

I believe one of the reasons God allowed Job and Joseph to suffer so much was because He knew that all kinds of diseases, natural disasters, and other tragedies would befall people. He wanted them to know it did not mean that they had offended Him. It did not mean that He had turned His back on them.

Joseph and Job also show us that life can turn on a dime for bad, but also for good. Do not lose faith in God or feel like He has abandoned you or your family in your hour of need.

Discussion Questions

1. Do you feel like you are being punished for something?

2. Have you asked God for forgiveness?

3. Guilt can make you feel unlovable. Do you feel like not even God could love you or forgive you?

4. What evidence do you have that that is true?

• • •

12

Moses in the Bulrushes:
God Saves a Baby and the Future

CHILDREN'S CLASS

Materials and Preparation

- A small plastic baby
- Numerous plastic Easter eggs or small boxes
- Treats to fill the eggs

Use the small plastic baby to represent baby Moses during circle time. He should then be hidden in a box or an egg for the children to search for. For the group project, fill many small boxes or eggs with treats, including one with the baby Moses inside. Hide the boxes and have the kids search for them. Have a meaningful prize for whoever finds baby Moses.

Rotate and add packet items as needed. Choose an appropriate video or CD to use during the lesson.

Lesson Objective

To teach the children that following God helps those around them.

Opening Prayer

The same opening prayer is prayed at the start of every lesson.

Circle Time

A Pharaoh was a leader of Egypt. Once there was a really mean one. He was afraid of people who were different from him and he tried to kill them, even the babies! Moses' mother loved him very much and did not want him to be killed. So she made a little basket and placed him into the water. She prayed that God would take care of him. God did! He sent Moses to the Pharaoh's daughter who loved little Moses. Moses grew up to free all the Israelites, but also to tell the world what God's law was. Moses forever changed the world.

When we place our lives and futures in God's hands and pray like Moses' mother did, God can do great things with us. We can change the world in little ways or maybe big ways, just like Moses did.

Scripture Reading

Using an ability-appropriate Bible, each aide should read the story of Moses to their student.

Packet Time

Time to work individually (with their aide) on the goal-oriented work provided in the packet.

Group Activity

Have the children search for the baby Moses hidden in the eggs or boxes.

Tell them they will keep all the treats they find and the one who finds baby Moses will get a special reward.

Video/Songs

Choose a thematically appropriate video or selection of songs. During this time, parents can meet for their Scripture study.

Closing Prayer

God, help us to keep searching until we find you.

Parents' Scripture Study

Individual Reading

Read Exodus 1 - 2:1-22

Selected Scripture

"When the child grew, she brought him to Pharaoh's daughter, who adopted him as her son and called him Moses; for she said, 'I drew him out of the water'" (Exodus 2:10).

Contemplation

Moses' mother saved her son by giving him away. Because of the political situation, she knew she could not raise him herself. She had to trust God to guide her son to the right person. Pharaoh's daughter in turn entrusted Moses to his mother. She trusted that she would return him when the time came.

Parents of children with autism can have an interesting partnership with their children's teachers and school districts. We do not always have the emotional, financial, educational, or material resources to give our children the intensive education that they need. We send them off to the school hoping and praying that they will get the proper care.

We try to advocate for them, but everything involves dealing with another person to get the proper care for our children. Some parents end up home schooling their children. Many parents cannot home school, and many others would not want to even if they could. Sooner or later we all reach the time when we must place our child in the basket and trust God for their care, first at school and finally at our death.

Discussion Questions

1. Do you trust your child's teachers?

2. How do you work out problems with them?

3. Do you envision a time when your child can live apart from you?

4. Are you working toward that goal?

• • •

13

Moses and the Burning Bush: God Calls Us as We Are

CHILDREN'S CLASS

Materials and Preparation

- Yellow and orange crepe paper
- Fan (make sure it's safe from little fingers)

During the group activity you will attach the crepe paper to the kids and have them walk in front of the fan, so they can look like a burning bush.

Rotate and add packet items as needed. Choose an appropriate video or CD to use during the lesson.

Lesson Objective

To reassure the children that we do not have to be perfect for God to use us.

Opening prayer

The same opening prayer is prayed at the start of every lesson.

Circle Time

You might think that God wants to use the smartest people or the strong, beautiful people, but God likes to use all kinds of people for his work — even people who think they're not smart or strong. Did you know that Moses had a hard time talking? It is true.

Here's what happened when God asked Moses to do something. God appeared to Moses in a burning bush. Moses was curious about the bush because it seemed to be on fire but it wasn't burning up. God then spoke to Moses. God asked Moses to go talk to the Pharaoh and the Israelites. Moses told God to please ask someone else. "I have always had trouble talking," Moses said. He thought he talked really slowly and that everything he said came out sounding stupid. But God saw inside Moses' heart and knew that Moses was the best person for such a big job.

Moses looked at what he could not do. God wanted Moses to look at what he could do with God's help. God let Moses bring his brother Aaron along to help him do the talking, but Moses was going to be God's miracle worker.

Everybody has problems. People do not need to be perfect for God to work with them. They only need to have a good heart and a willingness to follow Him.

Scripture Reading

Using an ability-appropriate Bible, each aide should read the story of the burning bush to their student.

81

Packet Time

Time to work individually (with their aide) on the goal-oriented work provided in the packet.

Group Activity

Use orange and yellow crepe paper to cover the children with the fire of God's love. Tell them God's fire is different from regular fire. Regular fire burns and hurts people. God's fire doesn't burn bushes or people. Only God can make God's fire.

Video/Songs

Choose a thematically appropriate video or selection of songs. During this time, parents can meet for their Scripture study.

Closing Prayer

God, set our hearts on fire with love of you. Help us serve you just the way we are.

PARENTS' SCRIPTURE STUDY

Individual Reading

Read Exodus 2:11 through 4:17.

Selected Scripture

"Moses, however, said to the Lord, 'If you please, I have never been eloquent, neither in the past, nor recently, nor now that you have spoken to your servant; but I am slow of speech and tongue'" (Exodus 4:10).

Contemplation

Ever feel unequal to the task of parenting your child? You are in good company. Most parents of children with disabilities feel that way. Moses felt that way when God gave him a huge task to do. We prefer to feel competent, to know that we are equal to the task before us. That gives us self-confidence, but it doesn't provide growth.

God is like the ultimate coach — always pushing us to do more than we thought possible. After we start learning His ways, we start developing God-confidence and there is tremendous growth. This growth is not just for ourselves but for all those around us. God did not push Moses just for Moses' sake; He did it for the sake of the Jewish people and all the people in the future.

When we pray, most of us usually ask God to help us accomplish our agenda. What we should pray is, "God, help us accomplish your agenda." Of course, this isn't as easy as it sounds on paper. In practice it's actually a lifetime of yielding our own hopes and dreams to God. It is willing ourselves to trust God even though we feel hysterical or distraught. This way of life is as far above our abilities to accomplish as freeing the Israelites was for Moses. The only way we can do this is through God doing it with us.

Discussion Questions

1. What are your hopes and dreams for your child?

2. What are your hopes and dreams for yourself?

3. Do you think that God might have bigger plans for your family?

4. How much control are you willing to yield to God?

• • •

Moses & Pharaoh:
Standing Up For Your Beliefs

Materials and Preparation

- 10 plague finger puppets (see Part One, Section D) or other symbols of the plagues

The finger puppets or other symbols of the plagues and used during circle time and during the group project. Find volunteers to perform the short skit of Moses and Pharaoh.

Rotate and add packet items as needed. Choose an appropriate video or CD to use during the lesson.

Lesson Objective
To teach the children that not doing what God wants causes problems.

Opening Prayer

The same opening prayer is prayed at the start of every lesson.

Circle Time

Moses did what God asked him to do. He and Aaron went before Pharaoh and asked him to let the Israelite people go. Pharaoh said no. So Moses showed Pharaoh some wonderful signs that God was with Moses, but Pharaoh still said no. Then God through Moses started sending plagues on Egypt. First all the water turned to blood, but Pharaoh still said no.

Then, one by one, God sent eight more plagues — frogs, gnats, flies, a sickness that affected all the animals, boils on people's bodies, hail, locusts, and complete darkness. Pharaoh would not let the Israelites go. He said no, even though his people were crying. The Israelites were not hurt by these plagues because God protected them. The tenth plague was the worst. God took all the firstborn boys. The people missed their boys and cried. Then Pharaoh finally said yes.

It is always better to say yes to God and obey Him. The more we sin and do wrong, the worse things get. God was going to save His people from this mean Pharaoh, no matter what it took. God will never stop trying to save us from evil. God also gives us chances to turn around and do what is right before sin destroys us.

Scripture Reading

Using an ability-appropriate Bible, each aide should read the story of the ten plagues to their student.

Packet Time

Time to work individually (with their aide) on the goal-oriented work provided in the packet.

Group Activity

Today, I am going to teach you a little song. For the adults this is to the tune of "Louie, Louie."

Here is how the words go: "Pharaoh, Pharaoh, whoa, oh. Let my people go. Yeah, yeah, yeah, yeah, yeah, yeah, yeah!"

Okay. Now I want you to sing it every time I ask you, "What did Moses say?"

Before we start singing we need two adults to read the parts of Moses and Pharaoh.

Okay, are you ready? "What did Moses say?" (Kids and adults sing.)

Moses: "God says, 'let my people go.'"

Pharaoh: (responds) "No."

Moses: "Then God will turn your water to blood."

Pharaoh: "Stop that. I'm sorry."

Moses: "God says, 'let my people go.'"

Teacher: "What did Moses say?" (Kids and adults sing.)

Pharaoh: "No."

Moses: "Then God will give you too many frogs."

Pharaoh: "There are too many frogs. Stop it. I'm sorry."

Moses: "God says, 'let my people go.'"

Teacher: "What did Moses say?" (Kids and adults sing.)

Pharaoh: "No."

Moses: "Then God will give you too many gnats."

Pharaoh : (swatting at gnats.) "Stop these gnats. I'm sorry."

Moses: "God says, 'let my people go.'"

Teacher: "What did Moses say?" (Kids and adults sing.)

Pharaoh: "No."

Moses: "Then God will give you too many flies."

Pharaoh: "Stop these flies; they are worse than the gnats. I'm sorry."

Moses: "God says, 'let my people go.'"

Teacher: "What did Moses say?" (Kids and adults sing.)

Pharaoh: "No."

Moses: "Then God will make your animals sick."

Pharaoh: "Stop that! All my animals are sick. I'm sorry."

Moses: "God says, 'let my people go.'"

Teacher: "What did Moses say?" (Kids and adults sing.)

Pharaoh: "No."

Moses: "Then God will give you painful itchy spots all over your body."

Pharaoh: (itching)"Stop this itching. It is driving me crazy. I'm sorry."

Moses: "God says, 'let my people go.'"

Teacher: "What did Moses say?" (Kids and adults sing.)

Pharaoh: "No."

Moses: "Then God will send down hail that will damage your plants and hurt you."

Pharaoh: (Avoiding pretend hail.) "Stop that hail. It hurts. I'm sorry."

Moses: "God says, 'let my people go.'"

Teacher: "What did Moses say?" (Kids and adults sing.)

Pharaoh: "No."

Moses: "Then God will send you locusts to eat all you plants."

Pharaoh: "Stop! The locusts ate all the food. I'm sorry."

Moses: "God says, 'let my people go.'"

Teacher: "What did Moses say?" (Kids and adults sing.)

Pharaoh: "No."

Moses: "Then God will send you a darkness that will last three whole days."

Pharaoh: "Stop! I am so mad at YOU for making things so bad. Go away."

Moses: "I will go away, but YOU have made things bad by not doing what God asked. He has one more plague. God will take your first born son and then you shall cry and beg my people to go."

Next week, we will learn about what happened on the night of the last plague.

Video/Songs

Choose a thematically appropriate video or selection of songs. During this time, parents can meet for their Scripture study.

Closing Prayer

God, help us to listen to you and obey you the first time you ask us to do something. Thank you for always trying to save us from evil.

PARENTS' SCRIPTURE STUDY

Individual Reading

Read Exodus 4:18-11.

Selected Scripture

"But Pharaoh's servants said to him, 'How long must he be a menace to us? Let the men go to worship the Lord, their God. Do you not yet realize that Egypt is being destroyed?'" (Exodus 10:7)

Contemplation

Pharaoh was stubborn and Moses was steadfast. What was the difference between the two? The differences were in their attitudes toward God, themselves, and their people.

Moses was a humble man, well aware of his weaknesses. He allowed God to work through him, with the glory going to God. He was steadfast in what he did, not letting himself be intimidated by Pharaoh or by the Israelites when they grumbled. What he did benefited his people.

Pharaoh was an arrogant man, a god unto himself. He took advice from nobody. He wanted all the glory and respect that man could give him. He would bend some when the going got tough but then would snap back and change his mind. He was not there to serve his people's needs. The people were there to serve his needs.

These different leadership styles can be observed in families as well. A family is dysfunctional if only one member's needs are being met. This can happen when a child has a disability. Everyone's needs are not going to be met unless there is a conscious effort to fill them. This includes our own needs.

We must be careful not to let our children turn into little pharaohs, calling all the shots. Often we are swayed by the grumbling or wrath of others. We need to stand firm like Moses and not be intimidated. For their own good, our children need to learn that other people's needs are important too. We should teach them the joy that can come from helping others.

The Israelites under the leadership of Moses were led into safety. The Egyptians under the leadership of Pharaoh suffered greatly. Which leadership style will you choose for your family?

Discussion Questions

1. Who best reflects your life right now? Pharaoh, Moses, the Egyptian servants, or the Israelites?

2. Whose needs are met best in your family?

3. Whose needs are met worst?

4. What would it take to make things more equitable?

5. Can you stand up for what is right against arrogance or grumbling?

• • •

15

Passover and the Red Sea: God Saves His People

MATERIALS

- Certificates and awards

- Party supplies or seder supplies

Have either a party like the Israelites had on the Red Sea shore or recreate a Seder. Give out certificates and awards to the kids.

Rotate and add packet items as needed.

Lesson Objective

To celebrate that God saved us.

Opening Prayer

The same opening prayer is prayed at the start of every lesson.

Circle Time

Last time we talked about all the plagues that God sent on Egypt — all the plagues except the last one. Today I will tell you what happened with the last plague. Remember, God was going to take all of the first-born boys. God told the Israelites, I do not want you to cry. So take a lamb and put its blood on your doorway. I will see the blood and the plague will pass over your house and your kids will be safe. He also told them to eat some unleavened bread and some bitter herbs. He wanted them to be dressed and ready to go because they would be leaving Egypt in the morning! So they all ate a big Passover meal and got ready to go.

The next morning Pharaoh was very sad and mad. He told them all to leave Egypt and so they did. But Pharaoh soon changed his mind again and told his soldiers bring the Israelites back.

Moses and the Israelites were up against the Red Sea and Pharaoh's soldiers were behind them when God told Moses to stretch out his staff over the waters. The Red Sea opened up, making dry land for the Israelites to escape. When the Egyptians tried to follow, the water flowed back. The Israelites were free!

God had saved them! Do you know what they did? They had a party, because God helped them. So that is what we are going to do at the end of class.

Scripture Reading

Using an ability-appropriate Bible, each aide should read the story of the Israelites' escape to their student.

Packet Time

Time to work individually (with their aide) on the goal-oriented work provided in the packet.

Group Activity

Party time! End of year party to celebrate God saving the Israelites and us. You can give out diplomas.

Closing Prayer

God, keep us safe and holy until we meet again.

Parents' Scripture Study.

Individual Reading

Read Exodus chapter 12 through chapter 15.

Selected Scripture

"They shall take some of its blood and apply it to the doorposts and lintel of every house in which they partake of the lamb. That same night they shall eat its roasted flesh with unleavened bread and bitter herbs" (Exodus 12:8-9)

"But the blood will mark the houses where you are. Seeing the blood, I will pass over you; thus, when I strike the land of Egypt, no destructive blow will come upon you" (Exodus 12:13).

Contemplation

God wanted to save the Israelites because they were his special people. He loved them very much. When God says, "You are my people," He wants a response. He wants to hear "And you are my God." When God reveals what he wants to do, he always asks us to respond. God made a covenant with Abraham and his descendents, and circumcision was to be the response. This became a way for the Israelites to say, "And you are my God."

On the night the plague came on the firstborn, God asked something more of the Israelites. He asked them to take a perfect lamb, sacrifice it, place its blood around their doors, and eat it up entirely, burning anything that is left. God also told them to make unleavened bread and bitter herbs. Their obedience to his requests would make the difference between life and death. On this night, the Israelites' response changed from, "and you are my God" to "and you are my God, my savior, and my Lord."

God also asked them to commemorate the Passover every year and to teach their children to do so. One of our most solemn duties as parents is to pass on our faith to the next generation. Your participation in this class has helped you to do just that. It has been my privilege to help you.

Discussion Questions

1. What is God calling you to do?

2. How do you express, "And you are my God"?

3. How have you and your children grown over the course of this Scripture study?

• • •

R

Resources

Children's Books & Other Materials

Children's books, teaching tools, and information about autism can be found in the following catalogs and websites:

❶ "Abilitations"
  Call 1-800-850-8602 or visit www.abilitations.com.

❷ Autism-Aspergers Publishing Co.
  Call 1-913-897-1004 or visit www.asperger.net.

❸ "Beyond Play"
  Call 1-877-428-1244 or visit www.beyondplay.com.

❹ "Different Roads to Learning"
  Call 1-800-853-1057 or visit www.difflearn.com.

❺ Future Horizons, Inc.
Call 1-800-489-0727 or visit www.FutureHorizons-autism.com.

❻ Jessica Kingsley Publications
Call 011-442-078332301 or visit www.jkp.com.

❼ Labosh Publishing
Call 1-717-898-3813 or visit www.laboshpublishing.com.

❽ Mayer-Johnson Co.
Call 1-800-588-4548 or visit www.mayer-johnson.com.

❾ Phat Art 4
Call 1-866-250-9878 or visit www.phatart4.com.

❿ "Pocket Full of Therapy"
Call 1-732-462-5888 or visit www.pfot.com.

⓫ "Special Needs Project"
Call 1-800-333-6867 or visit www.specialneeds.com.

⓬ Super Duper Publications
Call 1-800-277-8737 or visit www.superduperinc.com.

⓭ The Center for Speech and Language Disorders
Call 1-630-530-8551 or visit www.csld.com.

⓮ Woodbine House
Call 1-800-843-7323 or visit www.woodbinehouse.com.

Autism Resources

The ARC of the United States
Call 1-301-565-3842 or visit www.thearc.org.

Autism Research Institute
Fax 1-619-563-6840 or visit www.autism.com.

Autism Society of America
Call 1-800-3AUTISM or visit www.autism-society.org.

Bubel/Aiken Foundation
Call 1-224-430-0950 or visit
www.thebubelaikenfoundation.org/home.htm

Doug Flutie Jr. Foundation
Call 1-866-3AUTISM orVisit www.dougflutiejrfoundation.org.

Unlocking Autism
Call 1-866-366-3361 or visit www.unlockingautism.org/main.asp.

...

About the Author

Kathy Labosh graduated from Penn State and became an economist. She is now a stay-at-home mom to Sam and Nicky, both of whom are children with autism. It became her mission to help others in similar situations. Kathy formed a Special Education Religion Class and is the author of a specialized curriculum for children with autism, currently in development.

In 2004, Kathy published her first booklet in The Child with Autism series, THE CHILD WITH AUTISM GOES TO TOWN. Since then she has published two more booklets in the series. The Autism Society of America has endorsed the series and is the process of publishing it's own Child with Autism Series booklet, THE CHILD WITH AUTISM GROWS UP.

Ms. Labosh is also a speaker on the topic of autism. She spoke at the 2005 National Catholic Educators conference and has presented information to the ArchDiocese of Philadelphia. She frequently speak to groups near her home.

Kathy has also received an Honorable Mention for Children's Fiction from Writer's Digest.

LABOSH
BOOKLETS

Look for additional booklets in
The Child with Autism Series

The Child with Autism Goes to Town

Kathy Labosh
The Child with Autism
Goes to Town
The Go Anywhere Guide
250 tips for community outings

ISBN-13: 978-0-9744341-1-7 • US: $5.00 • CDN: $7.00
250 practical tips and helps per topic for fun & fearless
ventures with children who have autism. Includes:

- The Playground
- The Mall
- The Grocery Store
- Church
- Sporting Events
- The Dentist
- Fast Food Spots
- The Barbershop
- The Movie Theater
- The Amusement Park
- The Doctor
- The Library

All books include space on the front cover for your organization's information

The Child with Autism At Home

Kathy Labosh
The Child with Autism **at Home**
The Home-Life Guide
350 tips for work & play

ISBN-13: 978-0-9744341-2-4 • US: $6.00 • CDN: $8.00
300 practical tips & helps for happy living at home with
children who have autism. Includes:

- The Attic
- The Bedroom
- The Family Room
- The Music Room
- The Study
- The Broom Closet
- The Master Bedroom
- The Corner
- The Playroom
- The Kitchen
- The Bathroom
- The Front & Back Door

The Child with Autism Goes to Florida

Kathy Labosh
The Child with Autism
Goes to Florida
Theme Park & Resort Guide
Tips and Ride Reviews

ISBN-13: 978-0-9744341-3-1 • US: $9.95 • CDN: $12.95
Hundreds of practical tips & reviews of theme parks,
rides, & resorts for worthwhile exploration of central
Florida with children who have autism. Includes:

- Travel Web Searches
- Resort Safety
- Islands of Adventure
- Magic Kingdom
- Animal Kingdom
- Sea World
- Tickets
- Lost Children
- Universal Studios
- Disney-MGM Studios
- EPCOT
- Busch Gardens

Helping Families Living with Autism
www.laboshpublishing.com

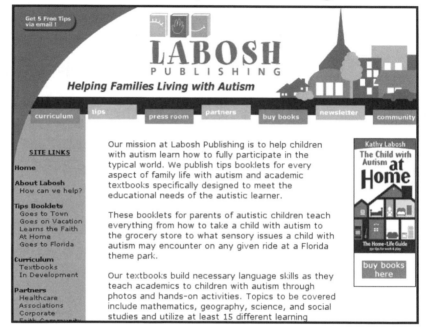

Labosh Publishing was founded in 2003, by a mother and a couple of special education teachers who wanted to improve the lives of children with autism and their families. Visit www.laboshpublishing.com for a wealth of information and resources.

- ❧ **Get free tips**
- ❧ **Order books online**
- ❧ **See what's new & upcoming**
- ❧ **Check out links to helpful sites**
- ❧ **Free Quarterly Newsletter**
- ❧ **Discover ways to connect to the autism community**